This book belongs to

_ _ _ _ _ _ _ _ _ _ _ _

Quiet Ninja

By Mary Nhin

Pictures by
Jelena Stupar

Mrs. Smith is my favorite teacher. We have a routine when we enter her classroom. She sings a line to the tune of "Mickey," and we respond by singing a line back.

Would you like to try it? It goes like this...

Personally, I haven't always had this awesome capability to control my volume.

If I was walking down the hall in school, you could have mistaken me for a giant from all the noise I made.

While in the car traveling, I would argue loudly with my sister.

At a restaurant with my family, I wouldn't know how to control my noisy tendencies.

Then one day, Innovative Ninja showed me how I could harness an underused superpower that I didn't even know I had.

To use our Ninja Toes and Ninja Voice, we can tiptoe and whisper. The goal is to be stealthy and camouflaged. That means we have to blend in and be hard to see.

NINJA TOES

When the noise level comes from heavy feet running and jumping, try tiptoeing.

NINJA VOICE

A ninja uses soft whispering so others can't see or hear them.

When I went to school the next day, I practiced my superpower of quiet.

I pretended I was walking on clouds on my way to the cafeteria. Using my Ninja Toes while walking through the hallways helped me to not be noticed.

In the library, I used a gentle voice to talk. With a Ninja Voice,
I was able to camouflage and not be heard or seen.

At home when everyone was relaxing, I remembered to be mindful of the noise I made, so that everyone could enjoy their evening. I was a Quiet Ninja, using my Ninja Voice and Ninja Toes.

I was able to tap into my quiet superpower
more than just that one day.

I continue to use my Ninja Toes and Ninja Voice every day in my life. Now, I know how to be a Quiet Ninja when I need to be!

Remembering to use your Ninja Toes and Ninja Voice could be your secret weapon in building your superpower of quiet.

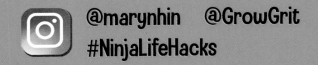

Made in the USA
Columbia, SC
15 June 2023

18129384R00020